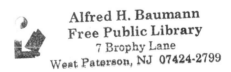

New Jersey
Plants & Animals

Mark Stewart

Heinemann Library
Chicago, Illinois

Designed by Heinemann Library
Page layout by Wilkinson Design
Printed and bound in the United States by
    Lake Book Manufacturing, Inc.

08 07 06 05 04
10 9 8 7 6 5 4 3 2 1

**Library of Congress
Cataloging-in-Publication Data**

Stewart, Mark, 1960-
    New Jersey plants and animals / Mark Stewart.
        v. cm. -- (State studies)
Includes bibliographical references (p. 47).
Contents: New Jersey's rich habitats -- New Jersey
animals and plants --
Endangered species of New Jersey -- Extinct
animals of New Jersey -- New
Jersey then and now -- Map of New Jersey --
Timeline.
    ISBN 1-4034-0676-6 (lib. bdg.) --
ISBN 1-4034-2685-6 (pbk.)
    1. Zoology--New Jersey--Juvenile literature.
    2. Botany--New
Jersey--Juvenile literature. [1. Zoology--New Jersey.
2. Botany--New Jersey.] I. Title. II. Series.
    QH105.N5S74 2003
    578'.09749--dc21

2003010356

Some words are shown in bold, **like this.** You can find out what they mean by looking in the glossary.

Acknowledgments
The author and publishers are grateful to the
following for permission to reproduce copyright
material:

Cover photographs by (main) Kelly-Mooney
Photography/Corbis; (row, L-R) Gene Ahrens, Joe
McDonald/Corbis, Joe McDonald/Corbis, David
Muench/Corbis

Title page (L-R) Steve Maslowski/Photo Researchers,
Inc., John Serrao/Photo Researchers, Inc., Breck P.
Kent/Animals Animals; contents page (L-R) Robert J.
Ashworth/Photo Researchers, Inc., Joe McDonald/
Corbis; p. 4t William H. Mllins/Photo Researchers, Inc.;
pp. 4b, 16t Jim Zipp/Photo Researchers, Inc.; p. 6
Richard Kolar/Animals Animals; p. 7t Steve Maslowski/
Photo Researchers, Inc.; pp. 7b, 17t John Serrao/
Photo Researchers, Inc.; p. 8 The Granger Collection,
New York; p. 9 E. R. Degginger/Color Pic, Inc. ;
p. 10t Bob Stovall/Bruce Coleman Inc.; p. 10b
Michael P. Gadomski/Photo Researchers, Inc.; pp. 12,
27b Joe McDonald/Animals Animals; p. 13t E. R.
Degginger/Animals Animals; p. 13b John Foster/
Masterfile; p. 14 David Muench/Corbis; p. 15 John W.
Bova/Photo Researchers, Inc.; p. 16b Lynda
Richardson/Corbis; pp. 17b, 19 Corbis; p. 18 Daniel
Hulshizer/AP Wide World Photo; p. 20 Bryan Knox/
Papilio/Corbis; p. 21t Richard Kolar/Earth Scenes;
pp. 21b, 37 Jeff Lepore/Photo Researchers, Inc.; p. 22
Richard T. Nowitz/Corbis; pp. 23, 32b, 44b
Bettmann/Corbis; pp. 24, 41 Doug Wechsler/Earth
Scenes; p. 25 George McCarthy/Corbis; pp. 26, 44t E.
R. Degginger/Photo Researchers, Inc.; p. 27t Robert J.
Ashworth/Photo Researchers, Inc.; p. 28 E. R.
Degginger/Earth Scenes; p. 29 Donna McWilliam/AP
Wide World Photo; p. 30 Karen Carr; p. 32t David
Grimaldi/American Museum of Natural History/AP
Wide World Photo; p. 33 Stouffer Productions/Animals
Animals; p. 34 National Park Service/AP Wide World
Photo; p. 35 Merlin D. Tuttle/Bat Conservation
Intl./Photo Researchers, Inc.; p. 38t Joe McDonald/
Corbis; p. 38b Gilbert S. Grant/Photo Researchers,
Inc.; p. 39t John Lemker/Photo Researchers, Inc.;
p. 39b L. West/Photo Researchers, Inc.; p. 40t M. T.
Frazier/PSU/Photo Researchers, Inc.; p. 40b Breck P.
Kent/Animals Animals; p. 42 Kelly-Mooney
Photography/Corbis

Photo research by John Klein

Special thanks to expert reader Chad Leinaweaver,
the Director for the Library at The New Jersey
Historical Society, for his help in the preparation
of this book.

Special thanks to Deborah Mercer of the New
Jersey State Library for her help in map research.

Every effort has been made to contact copyright
holders of any material reproduced in this book.
Any omissions will be rectified in subsequent
printings if notice is given to the publisher.

Contents

Wild New Jersey

Although New Jersey has a total area of just 8,200 square miles, it is home to a variety of **ecosystems.** This is because New Jersey has many physical regions—from mountains in the northwest to coastline in the east and south. Each region creates its own **diverse** ecosystems.

New Jersey, the fifth-smallest state, has the greatest wildlife variety per square mile of any state. It has 90 **species** of mammals, 79 species of reptiles and **amphibians,** more than 400 kinds of fish, and 322 species of birds.

New Jersey is also the land of second chances. In the more than 350 years since Europeans first settled in the

Birds gather on the shore (below) *in Reeds Beach, New Jersey. A young bald eagle* (right) *waits for its parents to bring food.*

New Jersey Ecosystems

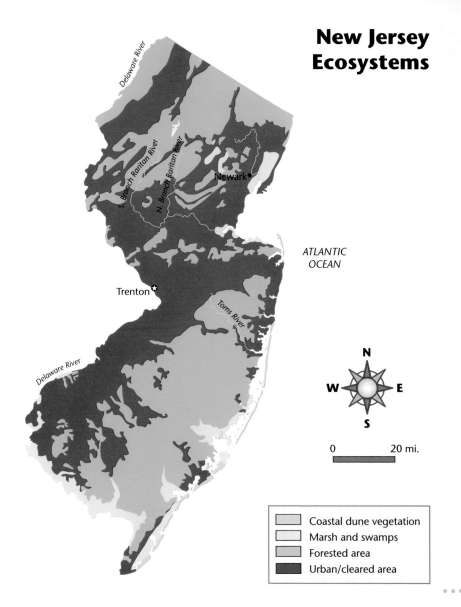

Coastal dune vegetation
Marsh and swamps
Forested area
Urban/cleared area

New Jersey's many towns and cities make up a large portion of the state. It has the highest percentage of people living in **urban** *areas in the United States.*

area, several major species have been wiped off the map—only to return. For example, the bald eagle returned to New Jersey in the 1970s, and its population increased steadily into the 1990s.

WHITE-TAILED DEER

There are more white-tailed deer in New Jersey than any other large **mammal.** The white-tailed deer has a tail that is brown on top and white on the bottom and sides. When it runs, it raises its tail so the last thing to be seen before it disappears into the trees and brush is a bright, white puff of fur. Female deer have between one and three young fawns a year and stand about five feet tall. Males are a foot

The average white-tailed deer stands about 3.5 feet tall at the shoulder and weighs between 400 and 500 pounds.

taller and have pronged, or forked, antlers. Male deer use these antlers in fighting matches to win control of a group.

During the 1700s and 1800s, when people cleared forests for farming, the deer **population** greatly increased. Deer eat shrubs and other low-growing plants, the type of plants that usually grows in these newly created openings. Because at that time there were no laws banning deer hunting, the settlers killed many deer to keep them off the farmland.

By the end of the 1800s, the white-tailed deer had been hunted to near **extinction** in the state. However, two New Jersey families had private **game preserves** that included herds of white-tailed deer. New Jersey's many deer can be traced to these herds. The state bought several of the deer and set them free in parks and forests, while others were set free by their owners.

The number of deer has increased so much in recent years that it is not unusual to see large herds grazing in open fields or standing wide-eyed at the edges of roads and highways. Now, with more people moving into New Jersey's pastureland and forests, the number of deer may begin to decrease. However, some herds of deer are being squeezed into forests that are surrounded by private homes and businesses. Because animals cannot be hunted in these areas, their numbers have exploded, and they have begun

eating the plants from people's gardens. This in turn may have led to a rise in cases of Lyme disease in people. Lyme disease is passed from deer to humans by the bite of a tick. Such issues have caused conflicts between homeowners and animal rights groups.

The goldfinch is about five inches long, just slightly longer than a child's hand.

THE GOLDFINCH

The official state bird of New Jersey is the goldfinch, also known as the wild canary. It is a chirpy yellow-and-black bird, with a sweet song. The goldfinch helps to control several damaging insects. It seems to enjoy feeding close to humans. The goldfinch is most noticeable in the early days of summer, when other birds are busy preparing their nests or raising their young. The goldfinch lays its eggs and raises its young later in the warm-weather months. So, for several weeks in June and July it sometimes seems to have the sky to itself.

THE VIOLET

New Jersey's state flower is the violet. Violets are found in wooded areas throughout the state. They grow in moist, shady areas. Violets have smooth, glossy, heart-shaped leaves and five-petaled flowers.

The meadow violet ranges in color from white to deep violet.

Forests

Forests cover about two-fifths of New Jersey. This **ecosystem** is found mainly in northern and southeastern New Jersey. New Jersey's forests include more than 200 different **species** of trees. Almost half of New Jersey's forests are part of state forests, parks, and other public lands.

USEFUL FORESTS

In the 1600s, when European settlers first came to New Jersey, it was wooded with tall, mature trees. The only breaks in the forest occurred where the **native** people had cleared land for farming. The trees' straight trunks were perfect for building log cabins and fences. New Jersey's towering white pines also made excellent masts for ships. The turpentine, tar, and resin that came from the tree sap also proved important to the shipping **industry.**

This 1824 engraving shows how European settlers used New Jersey's forests for building houses.

As New York City and Philadelphia started to grow in the 1700s, demand increased for New Jersey's lumber, which also included oak, ash, maple, and hickory. When the state's iron industry began to grow in the 1800s, more wood was used for fuel. When the railroads began operating, the demand for wood grew even higher. As a result, by the mid-1800s almost every tree that was standing when people first settled in New Jersey in 1664 had been cut down.

Settlers used oaks, such the one above, for homebuilding.

About 100 years ago, a traveler in New Jersey would have found a state without tall trees. The situation began to improve during the Great Depression, a period of economic hardship that lasted from 1929 to 1939. One of the ways the government kept people working was to create the Civilian Conservation Corps (CCC). The CCC put many young men to work planting trees around New Jersey. Today, 214 tree species grow in the state, and once again there are mature forests throughout New Jersey.

PLANTS OF THE FOREST

Hardwood forests are found in the northern part of New Jersey. They include beech, birch, maple, oak, and yellow-poplar trees. Cedars, oaks, and pitch-pines grow in New Jersey's southern forests.

The red oak (top right) is the official state tree of New Jersey. The dogwood (above) is the official state memorial tree of New Jersey.

THE RED OAK

The red oak often grows to 100 feet or more, and in the fall its leaves turn a deep shade of red. The red oak's acorns are oblong, with shallow, saucer-like cups that are reddish-brown. Its trunk is dark, with shiny ridges

THE DOGWOOD

Depending on its location, the dogwood can be more like a bush, at only 10 feet high, or stand as tall as 40 feet. It has clustered white flowers and hard, close-grained wood. Its wood has been used for everything from tool handles to golf club heads. In addition, its fruit is an important source of food for several animals, including deer, rabbits, and songbirds.

ANIMALS OF THE FOREST

Many **species** of animals make their home in New Jersey's forests. Deer, raccoons, bears, bobcats, and many kinds of birds feed on the nuts, plants, and fruit found there. They are all part of the **food web** in this **habitat.** New Jersey's forests have many **food chains**

*Every habitat in New Jersey has a specific food web. If any plant or animal within that food web should die out, the others could become **threatened** as well.*

and food webs. A food chain shows how different plants and animals in a habitat rely on one another for food. One species becomes food for another. When food chains combine, a food web is created.

BLACK BEARS

The black bear is New Jersey's largest land **mammal.** Despite the state's large **population,** this creature is **thriving** in forested areas throughout the northern section of the state. Black bears grow up to 6 feet tall and can weigh more than 300 pounds. They live about 30 years and prefer to eat fruits, nuts, grasses, and, of course, honey. If they are really hungry, they will hunt smaller animals.

In 2001, more than 1,100 black bears roamed New Jersey.

Black bear cubs stay with their mother for two years. By the time they go out on their own, they are strong and trained in the ways of the woods. If a mother loses her cubs to an accident, she can start a new family almost immediately. In this way, the black bear population is able to bounce back from many natural or human-made troubles.

One hundred years ago, however, the black bear was almost **extinct** in New Jersey. As settlers cleared the forests in the 1700s and 1800s, they drove the black bear north into New York and west into Pennsylvania. Settlers killed those remaining in New Jersey, not because they were dangerous but because they were considered pests. Only since the 1980s, as the state's northern forests have grown, did the black bear return.

PORCUPINES

Another mammal that is beginning to **thrive** again in New Jersey's forests is the porcupine. This slow-moving animal is an expert tree climber, and it defends itself with rows of sharp quills on its back, sides, and tail. These quills are actually stiff hairs with hooked ends. Although

Even though this one wandered out for a look around during the day, porcupines are actually nocturnal. That means they are usually active at night and sleep during the day.

the porcupine can shake them loose during an attack, it cannot shoot them, as people once believed. A member of the rodent family, it is more closely related to rats and squirrels than to beavers and woodchucks.

RED-HEADED WOODPECKERS

A bird that is pictured on many New Jersey license plates is the red-headed woodpecker. This bird is easy to recognize, with its black, white, and red feathers. It is even easier to hear as it pecks at tree limbs in its woodlands **habitat.** However, the disappearance of New Jersey's woodlands habitat is causing this birds' numbers to decrease.

About 180 species of birds are part of the woodpecker family.

During the late 1700s and 1800s, the red-headed woodpecker was a common and widespread **species** in the Northeast. It is now uncommon. Red-headed woodpeckers suffered population declines because of loss of habitat and places to build nests. People also killed them for their feathers, which were used to decorate women's hats. Farmers also killed red-headed woodpeckers because they damaged fruit and berry crops. Today, the species is considered to be rare in the Northeast and was listed as **threatened** in New Jersey in 1979.

Wetlands

Wetlands are places that are covered with shallow water much of the year or have water-logged soil. Marshes are wetlands in which thick, tall grasses grow. Swamps are wetlands in which trees grow. Wetlands are one of New Jersey's most-productive **ecosystems.** They are home to a large variety of plants and animals. Wetlands make up about nineteen percent of New Jersey's land area.

About two-thirds of New Jersey's wetlands are freshwater wetlands. They are generally found along lakes, rivers, and streams. About one-third of the state's wetlands are saltwater marshes. These wetlands are generally found near the ocean coast. A variety of birds, **mammals,** reptiles, and **amphibians thrive** in this **habitat.**

White Cedar Swamp is one of the few wetlands left in New Jersey.

BIRDS

Wetlands are a favorite spot for **migrating** birds and a favorite spot for bird-watchers. Common wetland birds in New Jersey include great blue herons, red-tailed hawks, red-winged blackbirds, and wood ducks. Some of the **species** that New Jersey bird-watchers prize most highly are the black skimmer, northern harrier, piping plover, and bobolink, because these species are now in decline as a result of disappearing wetland and beach nesting areas.

Some **birds of prey,** on the other hand, seem to be doing fine. Birds such as eagles, owls, and ospreys have increased their **populations** over the last twenty years. Poisons and other forms of pollution in the **food chain** had robbed these birds of their ability to raise chicks successfully. However, new laws banning the release of certain chemicals into the water have corrected this problem.

Although migration occurs all year, two periods are particularly good for bird-watching. The first period runs from late April to late May, and the second begins in early September and runs through early October. The best places to see these birds are in wetland areas, such as the Delaware Bayshore and Gateway National Recreation Area of Sandy Hook.

Big Day for the Birds

New Jersey's huge **population** of **migrating** birds draws bird-watchers from all over the world. Once seen, the flyaways in the spring and fall are not easily forgotten. Like clockwork, entire species lift off from New Jersey's shores and marshes and continue on to their summer or winter homes.

There are so many birds to see that in 1984 the state began a program called the World Series of Birding. It is a 24-hour event held each May in which teams see how many **species** they can identify by sight or sound. The clock starts and ends at midnight, so everything from owls to eagles to shore birds is fair game. The Audubon Society hosts the World Series of Birding.

AMPHIBIANS, REPTILES, AND MAMMALS

Amphibians are common animals found in New Jersey's wetlands. These animals count on the wetlands for **breeding** because they lay their eggs in the wet areas. Some common amphibians of New Jersey's wetlands include the spotted salamander, the wood frog, the bullfrog, the northern spring peeper, and the northern gray tree frog.

Salamanders eat insects, worms, snails, and other small animals, including members of their own species.

The northern gray tree frog is not easy to find. It can change the color of its skin to blend in with its surroundings. It usually lives near the tops of trees. The best chance of spotting one is during late April, when it comes down to mate and lay its eggs in puddles. In the winter, the northern gray is able to survive thanks to a special chemical it produces. The chemical allows the frog to partially freeze and then thaw out in the spring.

Most tree frogs are less than four inches in length.

Reptiles also live in New Jersey's wetlands. Snakes and lizards like to live in the drier parts, such as under a fallen log. Turtles, on the other hand, prefer living near water. New Jersey's reptiles include the common snapping turtle, the spotted turtle, the northern fence lizard, the eastern garter snake, and the eastern hognose snake.

MAMMALS

Many kinds of **mammals** also live in New Jersey's wetlands. They include muskrats, beavers, otters, and raccoons. A river otter has a slender body, a long neck, small ears, and short legs. The head is flattened, and the base of the tail is nearly as thick as the body. Otters have webbed feet and can swim underwater for about one-fourth of a mile without

Otters are playful as adults. A favorite activity is sliding down a bank of mud or snow and plunging into water or a snowdrift.

coming up for air. Though otters like to travel by water, they can move on land faster than the average adult can run. Their food consists of small water animals, including fish.

FISH

The waters in New Jersey's wetlands support more than 30 **species** of freshwater sport fish, including record-sized perch, pickerel, and salmon. The state releases trout into rivers and streams for fishing. The most popular freshwater fish is the small-mouth bass. Each spring, there is a world-famous shad run in the Delaware River. Shad are anadromous fish. This means they are born in rivers and then **migrate** to the ocean, where they spend most of their lives. In 2001, more than 400,000 shad migrated from the ocean to the

Anglers fish for shad during their annual return to the river in which they hatched. The shad return to begin their reproduction cycle again.

rivers in which they hatched, traveling upstream as the water warms to about 55°F.

PLANTS OF THE WETLANDS

The plants that live in New Jersey's wetlands have **adapted** to the conditions of this **ecosystem.** These plants often grow in standing water. Plants such as phragmites, or reeds, and cattails have developed long tubes that they use to get oxygen from above the water to carry down to the roots that are below the water. Some wetland plants, such as the water lily, have adapted in such a way that they float on shallow water.

Cattails typically rise about eight feet out of the water.

The Coast

New Jersey has about 130 miles of ocean coastline, from Sandy Hook to Ocean City. But it has about 1,800 miles of shoreline because of the many small barrier islands off the coast.

Sandy beaches and dune **habitats** are found where the ocean meets the land. Sometimes the tide washes over them. Beach plants, such as dune grasses, hold up well under these harsh conditions.

The American oystercatcher eats oysters, clams, and mussels. It attacks them when their shells are exposed and still partially open.

New Jersey's beaches provide a feeding area for thousands of shorebirds. Birds such as the common tern and the American oystercatcher survive by feeding on insects and fish. Dunes provide nesting places for these birds.

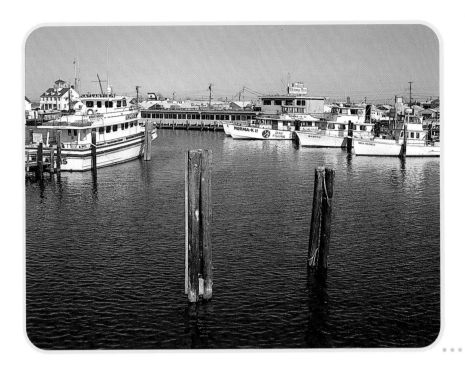

Fishing boats lay at anchor in Point Pleasant, New Jersey. The state's commercial fish catch is worth about $100 million annually.

AQUATIC LIFE

New Jersey's coastal waters support a great variety of **aquatic** life. More than 60 **species** of fish live in the coastal waters, ranging from huge 1,000-pound bluefin tuna to delicate blowfish. The favorites of anglers are the fluke, flounder, bluefish, weakfish, and striped bass that swim off the Atlantic beaches and in the coastal rivers.

More than 30 **marine mammals** have been spotted in New Jersey coastal waters. Among the most common marine mammals are the harbor seal and the bottle-nosed dolphin. A bottle-nosed dolphin grows to a length of about nine feet and can weigh as much as 1,400 pounds. Sometimes they can be seen jumping just a few yards from New Jersey's beaches.

Two of the state's most famous marine animals are the horseshoe crab and blue claw crab. Horseshoe crabs have been around since before the age of the dinosaurs, millions of years ago. Each spring, they arrive in large numbers at

Horseshoe crabs in Cape May come ashore to lay their eggs.

The Daily Grind

In the mid-1800s, New Jerseyans started harvesting horseshoe crabs, taking over one million a year. At first, they were ground up and used to feed hogs. But when it was discovered that they were a rich source of **nitrogen,** horseshoe crabs were used as **fertilizer.** A **thriving** business sprang up in Cape May, where so many of these creatures laid their eggs. Crab farmers waited until the crabs had deposited their eggs, then set up fences to herd the crabs into holding pens. The farmers then plucked the crabs out of the water and turned them into a fertilizing powder. This practice went on for more than 100 years before the state began to protect the horseshoe crab.

the area around Cape May to lay their eggs in the sand. For this reason, New Jersey's coast is a stopping point for many millions of **migrating** birds, which feed on the many eggs.

The blue crab is one of the most common sea creatures in the western Atlantic Ocean. The blue crab's shell is a

A boy holds up his prize catch—a blue crab.

Jersey Jaws

One of the most famous series of American shark attacks happened during a ten-day period in the summer of 1916 at the Jersey Shore. Four people were killed and one was badly injured. The first two attacks took place near the beach, while the others happened in Matawan Creek. The incidents set off a wave of panic that captured the world's attention.

It was once believed that a single white shark was responsible for the attacks. But scientists think it could have been three different sharks, possibly from three different species, including a tiger shark and a bull shark. White Sharks are rare near New Jersey's beaches. Bull sharks are more common and have been known to hunt in the mouths of rivers—and even swim upstream.

To this day, the 1916 shark attacks captivate New Jerseyans. In fact, a 2002 book entitled *Close to Shore* that told of the attacks became a best-seller!

blend of olive-green, blue, and red, and it can grow up to eight inches in length. The blue crab feeds on the bodies of dead animals.

Many people treasure the blue crab for its sweet taste. As a result, crabbing is a popular family outing along the Jersey Coast. More than half of the crab harvest takes place in Barnegat Bay, Little Egg Harbor, and the Maurice River **estuary.** Crabbing accounts for almost one-third of the recreational fishing activity in the state.

The Pine Barrens

New Jersey's Pine Barrens region is located in the southern part of the state. It is one of the most unique **ecosystems** in the country. Its sandy, **acidic** soil covers more than 1.4 million acres, about one-fourth of New Jersey's land area. It is the largest tract of open space on the mid-Atlantic coast. In 1983, the Pine Barrens was designated a Biosphere Reserve by the the United Nations Educational, Scientific, and Cultural Organization (UNESCO).

The Batsto River flows through the Pine Barrens in the Wharton State Forest.

PLANTS

The Pine Barrens's pine, oak, and cedar trees and its streams and ponds support a variety of plant

life—between 800 and 850 different plant **species.** The Pine Barrens is also home to more than 55 plant species that do not grow anywhere else in the state. Only the Pine Barrens and northwest New Jersey are home to a species of pitch pine and scrub oak that cannot be found anywhere else in the Northeast. These trees do not grow in the North except for a few places in Pennsylvania.

*The bog asphodel is listed on New Jersey's **endangered** plant species list.*

Fires caused by lightning are an important part of the Pine Barrens ecosystem. They help the ecosystem to be reborn. The heat from the fires causes the cones of the pitch pines to release their seeds. The seedlings then sprout in the soil, which has been enriched by the ash from the fire.

One interesting species of tree in the Pine Barrens is the pygmy pine, also called the dwarf pine. These trees are so short—sometimes only three to four feet tall—that it is easy to stand on a higher point and look over the trees for several miles.

In addition, the Pine Barrens are home to a variety of wildflowers. They include the pink lady's slipper orchid, the swamp pink lily, and the northern pitcher plant. The pitcher plant is unique because it relies on insects for part of its food. A few species of wildflowers in the Pine Barrens are rare. Some, such as the bog asphodel, are found nowhere else in the world.

FISH AND AMPHIBIANS

The fish and **amphibian species** that **thrive** in the Pine Barrens do so because they are able to breed in the **acidic** water in the ponds and streams. This means that these animals are unique to the Pine Barrens because these conditions do not exist anywhere else in New Jersey. The Pine Barrens tree frog and carpenter frog, for example, can lay their eggs in waters that would kill off the eggs of other species.

Anglers often use the minnow as live bait, and people sometimes raise minnows for this purpose.

Among the unusual fish in the Pine Barrens is the blackbanded sunfish, which lives its entire life in the area's ponds and streams. The eastern mudminnow can be found elsewhere in the state, but it is most common in the Pine Barrens. When the **water table** drops—usually in the summer months—this fish can survive out of water for extended periods thanks to a special part in its body that allows it to breathe air. The chain pickerel also lives elsewhere but has **adapted** to thrive in the Pine Barrens. Its duck-billed snout is designed for snapping up smaller fish. But because its normal **prey** cannot survive in the acidic water, it uses its jaws to go after dragonfly **larvae** and crayfish.

REPTILES

Of all the creatures of the Pine Barrens, reptiles seem to be the most common. Turtles, snakes, and lizards do very well in this **habitat.** There are plenty of insects,

plants, and bird eggs to eat, a wide range of vegetation to use for cover, and the sandy soil is excellent for **burrowing.** Although there are no reptiles that are unique to the Pine Barrens, many **threatened** species, including the eastern corn snake, thrive in this region.

MAMMALS

About two dozen species of **mammals** thrive in the Pine Barrens, including the white-tailed deer, gray fox, raccoon, red squirrel, and eastern cottontail. These are probably the five easiest to see. Harder to spot are the southern flying squirrel, beaver, river otter, and longtailed weasel.

The flying squirrel does not actually fly, but it can glide for almost 1,500 feet—that is the length of about five football fields.

Berry Nice

As long as there have been humans in southern New Jersey, cranberries have been an important crop. The Lenape people relied on cranberries for food, medicine, and clothing dye. Early settlers admired the vine's pink blossoms and likened them to the head of a crane. The name "crane berry" was later shortened to cranberry.

Cranberries grow on vines in wet, sandy, **acidic** soil. They occur naturally in the Pine Barrens and have been farmed in the surrounding areas since the 1830s. Some of the cranberry **bogs** in southern New Jersey are run by the same families that started them more than 150 years ago. Farmers use more than 6,000 acres of New Jersey's land for growing cranberries.

Cranberry sauce has been an important part of the Thanksgiving table for about 85 years. It was invented in New Jersey by farmer Elizabeth Lee, who called it Bog Sweet. She went into business with Marcus Urann of Massachusetts, and the company they started is now called Ocean Spray.

BIRDS

About 50 **species** of birds are common to the Pine Barrens. Many birds that visit this region keep moving because of a lack of nesting locations and a narrow range of feeding opportunities. One that has made the Pine Barrens its home, however, is the chatty little rufous-sided towhee.

Devil of a Dilemma

New Jersey's most famous animal, the Jersey Devil, is more **myth** than **mammal.** No one has ever killed or captured one of these creatures, and it has never been photographed. Yet, for hundreds of years people have described a dragonlike animal with the head of a horse, body of a serpent, wings of a bird, and claws of a dinosaur.

Many people have believed in and feared the Jersey Devil, and some have reported seeing it. In 1909, there were so many sightings that the Jersey Devil became a national news story. The Philadelphia Zoo offered $10,000 to

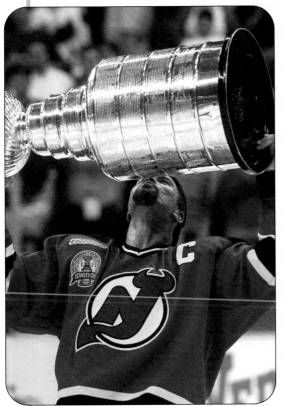

anyone who could trap the beast. Hoping to claim this prize, two New Jersey men kidnapped a kangaroo, painted stripes on it, and attached wings to its body. Their trick did not work.

Other reports of sightings happened in the 1950s and 1960s. Since then no one has seen the beast.

New Jerseyans are unable to say whether the Jersey Devil exists or not. However, they think that a monster living in their state is exciting. So exciting, in fact, that when it came time to name New Jersey's new National Hockey League (NHL) team in 1982, the overwhelming choice was the New Jersey Devils.

Whether a Pine Barrens species **thrives** and whether one does not depends largely on people's activities. During the last 200 years, humans have wiped out entire **populations** of plants and animals. But in recent years, with more awareness of the uniqueness and extreme sensitivity of the Pine Barrens, important steps have been taken to preserve and even improve this **habitat.**

Extinct Species

When New Jersey's first settlers found rocks in the mountains that contained **fossilized marine** life, they correctly figured that long ago the land was under water. In fact, New Jersey was completely covered with ancient oceans at least twice. Around 100 million years ago, the ocean laid down a greenish sand that contained the mineral glauconite. Early New Jerseyans knew that if they dug deep enough, they could take out this material—called marl—and use it to fertilize their crops. In 1838, a farmer was digging in a marl pit near Haddonfield when he hit something hard. It was a large

Pictured below is the hadrosaur as it may have looked when it roamed what is now New Jersey about 65 million years ago.

bone, and it looked ancient. Other people also discovered fossilized bones and took them home as souvenirs. They did not know they had dinosaur bones because no one had yet heard of a dinosaur!

THE HADROSAUR

Two decades later—in 1858—when the study of these ancient creatures was just beginning, a group from Philadelphia received permission to continue digging in the Haddonfield pit. They discovered the skeleton of a duck-billed dinosaur called a hadrosaur, which was originally called the Great Kangaroo Lizard. When scientists determined that certain pieces were missing, they went on a door-to-door search. They found the missing bones, some of which people were using as doorstops.

This was the first near-complete dinosaur ever found in the United States. It was also the first to be assembled, mounted, and displayed in public. The animal measured about 25 feet long, weighed 8 tons, and could walk on its hind legs. Because of the number of shells found with the bones, it was believed that the hadrosaur died in the shallow water where it fed, then drifted out to sea.

FOSSILS IN NEW JERSEY

New Jersey's fossils have provided important information about the **Cretaceous period.** Besides dinosaur bones, much plant material and many insects from this period have been preserved in amber, the **fossilized** sap of pine

Haddie Come Home

The peaceful plant-eating hadrosaur caused quite a stir when it was first displayed. But it was soon forgotten when other more exotic dinosaurs were found. It took an elementary school class from Westmont, New Jersey, to rediscover this treasure—on a class trip to Philadelphia, where the skeleton was on display. They launched a successful campaign to make "Haddie" the state dinosaur—the first one in the country. The only problem is, it is still in Pennsylvania!

trees. In fact, more **fossils** in amber have been found in New Jersey than in any other state. In recent years, the oldest known mushroom, ant, bee, flower, and feather have been found perfectly preserved in New Jersey amber. Several types of biting insects also have been found.

THE MASTODON

Another fossil that has turned up in various parts of what is today New Jersey is the mastodon. This large furry **mammal** looked much like an elephant. Ancient stories of huge beasts passed down by Native Americans suggest that mastodons were probably still here when the first humans arrived thousands of years ago. The first

The mastodon used its huge teeth—about three inches wide and six inches long—to chew the plants it ate.

mastodon discovery in New Jersey came in 1827 on a farm in Morris County. In 1972, a near-perfect skeleton was dug up in Sussex County. Scientists nicknamed it Matilda, and it is still on display in the state museum.

Like many of the large mammals that once roamed New Jersey, the mastodon was affected by climate change, changing **habitats,** and disease. When humans arrived with knowledge of how to hunt and kill this enormous beast, mastodons became **extinct.**

THE PASSENGER PIGEON

People were also responsible for a more recent extinction in New Jersey—the passenger pigeon. This bird once nested by the millions in the state's forests and provided the **native** people (and later European settlers) with an important source of food.

Passenger pigeons were easy to catch and kill, and flocks were so large that they could blot out the sun when they flew overhead. When these birds decided to roost, they would fill the branches of a forest for many miles. During colonial times, passenger pigeons were by far the most numerous birds in New Jersey. In the mid-1800s, passenger pigeons were still so plentiful that they were captured and used as live targets in carnival shooting galleries.

Scientists estimate that in the 1500s, between three billion and five billion passenger pigeons lived across eastern North America.

People were overhunting these birds. In addition, hunters began collecting passenger pigeon chicks. When the young were ready to leave

Cry Wolf

For thousands of years, the **native** people of New Jersey lived in harmony with wolves. They feared and respected these animals. However, there was enough land and enough large **game** so that people and wolves were not in competition and rarely came into direct contact. However, when European settlers began moving inland from New Jersey's coastal regions, the wolf population went into a steep decline.

Wolves require two things to survive: a good supply of large animals to hunt and territories that are free of people. As the settlers took more and more land for homes, farming, and **industry**—and as they hunted large game with guns—the wolves' **habitat** and food supply began shrinking. Forced to hunt and kill **domesticated** animals, wolves came into direct conflict with people and were quickly wiped out.

their nests, they would drop to the forest floor and look for food for a day or two before learning to fly. People would walk through the woods and pick up the chicks and drop them into sacks. Chicks still in their nests would be poked out with long sticks, or frightened into jumping with torches. The hunters would then grind them up for hog feed.

A decline in passenger pigeon chicks led to a decline in passenger pigeon adults. In many of the places where chicks were collected, the adults stopped nesting altogether. The passenger pigeon's survival depended on its vast numbers. Once the **population** fell below a certain point, they disappeared quickly. By the 1880s, the passenger pigeon was all but gone from New Jersey. The last bird died in an Ohio zoo in 1914.

Endangered Species

Although several **species** of animals and plants are in danger of disappearing from the state, only a handful are considered **endangered** by the federal government. These species are protected and, in some cases, programs to restore them have been very successful.

INDIANA BAT

New Jersey's only land **mammal** considered endangered by the federal government is the Indiana bat. It flies too fast to be identified in the night sky. The best time to see this animal would be while it is **hibernating.** But that is why it is endangered. A light sleeper, the Indiana bat is easily awakened from its winter slumber and will

When hibernating in caves, there can be as many as 300 Indiana bats per square foot!

starve to death if it cannot fall back to sleep. The bats who choose dead trees instead of caves are also in danger, because these trees are often cut down by humans.

BALD EAGLE

One of New Jersey's most successful wildlife programs has kept the bald eagle from becoming **extinct.** Between 100 and 125 bald eagles live in the state, with two-thirds of them in the southern half. Wildlife officials check their nests each winter and draw blood from chicks whenever possible to keep track of their health.

New Jersey's rich waters offer eagles a plentiful year-round food supply. It is also easy to see what originally destroyed these birds. Until recently, many New Jersey businesses dumped waste into rivers and streams. These poisonous chemicals entered the **food chain** and were present in the fish the eagles ate. This made the birds sick and prevented them from producing strong

U.S. Endangered Species in New Jersey

Plants

- Small-whorled Pogonia
- American chaffseed
- Seabeach amaranth
- Swamp pink
- Sensitive joint-vetch
- Bog Asphodel
- Knieskern's beaked-rush

Animals

- Bald eagle
- Indiana bat
- Northeastern beach tiger beetle
- Piping plover
- Dwarf wedgemussel
- Bog turtle

The bald eagle has been the U.S. national bird since 1782. Males have a wingspan of about 6.5 feet, while females' wings span nearly 8 feet.

eggs and healthy chicks. Polluted waters still keep some pairs from **breeding** successfully, particularly those in the Delaware Bay, but the situation is greatly improved.

ATLANTIC TURTLES

If you spend enough time on the beach, you might come across one of the five kinds of oceangoing turtles that swim off New Jersey's Atlantic coast. However, if a turtle is on the beach, it is probably sick, injured, or dead. The Atlantic hawksbill, loggerhead, ridley, and leatherback sea turtles are all on the **endangered** list. A fifth turtle, the Atlantic green, is technically a **threatened** species, because its numbers are declining.

Atlantic leatherbacks are the largest turtles in the world. They feed mainly on jellyfish, which has led to their decline. There are plenty of jellyfish off the Jersey coast, but there is also a lot of garbage that looks like a jellyfish. The leatherbacks swallow it, and the backward-pointing spines lining their throats make it difficult to cough this garbage back up. Swallowing plastic bags and balloons from birthday parties is a major problem.

The tree frog has sticky disks on the tips of its toes that help it to climb. It also has jewel-shaped eyes with gold- or copper-colored flecks.

PINE BARRENS TREE FROG

Among New Jersey's **endangered amphibians** is the Pine Barrens tree frog. Emerald green in color with purple, white, yellow, and orange markings, it measures just over an inch long and—as the name suggests—lives in the Pine Barrens region. The Pine Barrens tree frog is sensitive to even the smallest **environmental** change. Living in a state such as New Jersey, in which humans are constantly building homes, freeways, and malls, puts the tree frog and its environment at constant risk.

SHORTNOSE STURGEON

The shortnose sturgeon, which lives in the Hudson and Delaware Rivers, is the only New Jersey fish that is on the endangered **species** list. It was almost destroyed by **pollution** from upriver during the 1800s and 1900s, and its numbers were further reduced by a demand for sturgeon eggs. The shortnose sturgeon is anadromous, so it lives in saltwater (where the Hudson River meets the Atlantic Ocean) but lays its eggs in freshwater (in the northern part of the river) in the spring. Unlike most fish species, the shortnose sturgeon does not **breed** every

An adult male sturgeon can be as much as four feet long.

year. Males swim upriver to mate every year, while females lay eggs every three years. Newly hatched sturgeon are poor swimmers and tend to float along the bottom. If they make it to adulthood, however, they can live a very long time. One female is known to have reached her 67th birthday!

MITCHELL'S SATYR BUTTERFLY

The Mitchell's satyr butterfly is one of six endangered insects that makes its home in New Jersey. It is relatively small, with see-through wings and yellow-rimmed black eye spots. Each year, around July 1, it hatches in a handful of swamps and marshes in northern New Jersey and lives for only about ten days. As more and more people have come to live in these areas, collecting has taken a toll on the state's Mitchell's satyr colonies. They tend to fly slowly and low to the ground, which makes them easy to catch. The shrinking **habitat** of the Mitchell's satyr butterflies and pollution have also caused this species to become endangered.

The Chestnut Blight

One of the state's most common **hardwoods** was the American chestnut tree. It was a terrific shade tree and was perfect for home-building and furniture-making. It also produced a fruit that was loved by people as well as forest animals, including bears, deer, and several species of birds. During the 1920s and 1930s, a disease all but wiped out New Jersey's chestnut trees.

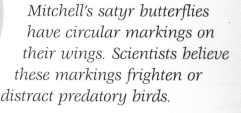

Mitchell's satyr butterflies have circular markings on their wings. Scientists believe these markings frighten or distract predatory birds.

The American burying beetle can smell a dead mouse as little as an hour after death, and from as much as two miles away!

AMERICAN BURYING BEETLE

The American burying beetle is also disappearing from the state, but no one is sure why. It is active at night and feeds by sniffing out its **prey,** burying it alive, and then eating its catch once it has suffocated. The burying beetle also lays its eggs inside dead animals, covering them with a sticky fluid from its mouth. When the eggs hatch, the babies feed on the dead animal. It is suspected that the American burying beetle's **habitat** is being destroyed, which would account for its decreasing numbers.

Happy Accidents

People's activities in the Pine Barrens has harmed many species. Between **pollution** and the destruction of habitats, many plants and animals have been pushed near **extinction.** However, humans have also added to the **diversity** of creatures in some cases. The digging of gravel pits, for example, has created catch basins for rainwater that is less acidic  than in other parts of the Pine Barrens. This has allowed species to breed where once they could not. Among the creatures that have benefited from people's activities in this way is the rare and **endangered** eastern tiger salamander.

New Jersey Then and Now

The wild areas of New Jersey have changed greatly over the past 350 years. Where wolves and panthers once outnumbered people, now there are eight million people and no **predators** larger than a coyote. Where magnificent forests once stood, now there are shopping malls, farms, office parks, and housing developments. Many **species** of plants and animals have been wiped out or **threatened.** The mission for the 2000s is to stop further destruction of important habitats and to strengthen and restore as many at-risk species as possible.

A new housing development in Avalon is built on some of New Jersey's precious wetlands.

PEOPLE AND THE ENVIRONMENT

The **environmental** pressure is most severe on the Jersey Coast, where the desires of vacationers and real estate developers meet head-on with the those trying to preserve natural beauty and animal **habitats.** In the last 30 years, the towns along the Atlantic Ocean have changed dramatically. At one time, they hosted weekenders and summer vacationers and remained quiet the rest of the year. Today, there has been an explosion of home-building sparked by an increased wave of full-time residents.

More people now want to use more of the beach more often. This could mean disaster for the state's **migrating** bird **species,** horseshoe crabs, and **marine mammals**— all of which depend on unpopulated stretches of shoreline to feed and reproduce. Meanwhile, right off the coast, there are signs that commercial and recreational fishing may be depleting the once-abundant marine life of New Jersey's waters. Runoff from new housing development and **pollution** from ships may be contributing to the problem, which is being closely watched.

Beachgoers crowd the sand in Point Pleasant on the Jersey Shore. Millions of people each year use the state's beaches.

New Jersey Wildlife Refuges

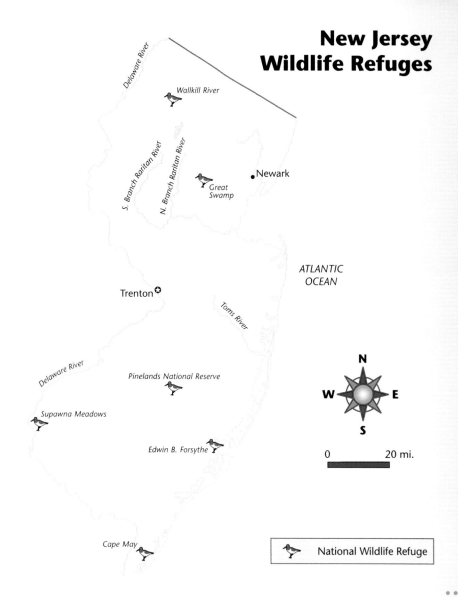

Wallkill River National Wildlife Refuge was established in 1990 and is the state's newest wildlife refuge.

From Sandy Hook down to Cape May, the state has set aside natural areas and made them off-limits to people during certain times of the year. New Jerseyans are hopeful that this will be enough to preserve the state's shore habitats.

NEW JERSEY'S WILDLIFE COMES BACK

One of the happier stories for New Jersey's wildlife is the comeback of white-tailed deer. New Jersey has also worked to restore and protect various **birds of prey,** including eagles, hawks, and falcons.

The beaver has made one of the best comebacks. The first fur-bearing creature to be wiped out by New Jersey

Female beavers have two to four babies at a time, which are usually born in April or May.

hunters, it disappeared from the state in the early 1800s. The beaver was in danger of being hunted to **extinction** elsewhere in the United States. But luckily for these animals, taste and fashion changed. For decades, beaver fur was used to make men's hats. But in the mid-1800s, silk became popular. Prices for beaver pelts hit rock bottom, and trappers finally left them alone. About 100 years ago, beavers raised for hunting purposes on private estates in northern New Jersey were released into the wild, and their numbers grew steadily. Today, the state's beaver **population** is actually increasing each year.

When it comes to supporting and preserving the plants and animals of New Jersey, New Jerseyans are finding ways to fix the problems. New Jerseyans are committed to finding a new balance between people and nature. In the process, many dying **species** will be saved, **threatened** species protected, and, most importantly, all species respected.

New Jerseyans, such as this man cleaning up a 1989 oil tanker spill, work hard to protect and preserve their state's wild places.

Map of New Jersey

0   20 mi.

New York

Pennsylvania

New Jersey

Atlantic
Ocean

Delaware

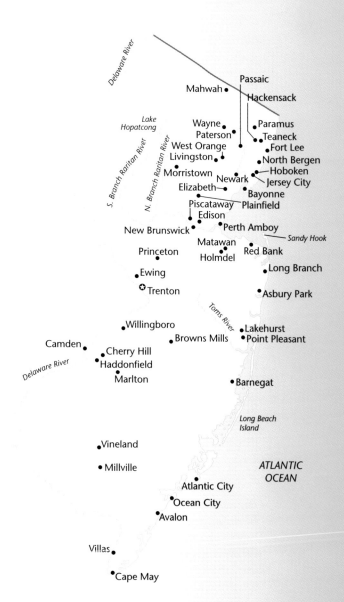

Delaware River

Passaic
Mahwah
Hackensack

Lake
Hopatcong
Wayne
Paterson
Paramus
Teaneck
West Orange
Fort Lee
S. Branch Raritan River
N. Branch Raritan River
Livingston
North Bergen
Morristown
Hoboken
Newark
Jersey City
Elizabeth
Bayonne
Piscataway
Plainfield
Edison
New Brunswick
Perth Amboy
Sandy Hook
Matawan
Princeton
Red Bank
Holmdel
Ewing
Long Branch
Trenton
Asbury Park

Toms River

Willingboro
Lakehurst
Browns Mills
Point Pleasant
Camden
Cherry Hill
Delaware River
Haddonfield
Marlton
Barnegat

Long Beach
Island

Vineland
ATLANTIC
OCEAN
Millville

Atlantic City
Ocean City
Avalon

Villas

Cape May

Glossary

acidic having a lot of acid. Few plants grow well in highly acidic soils.

adapted changed in order to live successfully in a certain habitat

amphibian an animal, such as a toad or frog, that lives in and around both water and land

aquatic living or found in water

bird of prey bird that feeds on meat that it hunts or finds

bog area of wet, spongy ground with unique types of plants

breeding giving birth to and raising young

burrowing digging underground to create a living place or to find food

Cretaceous period a long period in Earth's history that lasted from 145 million years ago to 65 million years ago

diverse/diversity made up of a lot of different parts or things

domesticated word that describes animals that people tame and raise for their own benefit. Cats, dogs, cows, and pigs are examples of domesticated animals.

ecosystem community of living things, together with the environment in which they live

endangered at risk of dying out

environment area where plants and animals live. The environment includes such conditions as land, water, soil, and climate.

estuary mouth of a river, where the saltwater tide flows in, and fresh and salt water mix

extinct/extinction no longer living on Earth

fertilizer something put into the soil to help plants grow

food chain diagram of the plants and animals that need one another for food within a single habitat

food web several food chains combined within an ecosystem

fossilized preserved, usually by turning to stone. Fossilized remains of animals and plants are called fossils.

game wild animals that are hunted by people for food or sport

game preserve area of land in which wild animals are protected

habitat place where an animal or plant lives and grows

hardwood type of tree that has hard wood. Maples, oaks, hickories, and elms are hardwoods.

hibernating entering a sleeplike state to avoid harsh living conditions. Most animals that hibernate do so in winter.

industry group of businesses that produce similar types of goods or services

larva young form of an insect, which looks like a worm and has no wings. Larvae is the plural form of larva.

mammal warm-blooded animal with a backbone. Female mammals produce milk to feed their young.

marine living in the ocean

migrate move from one place to another for food or to breed

myth mostly imaginary story that explains historical events or mysteries of nature

native originally from a certain area

nitrogen a natural substance that helps plants grow

pollution human-made wastes that harm the air, water, and soil

population the total number of people or other living things in a certain area

predator animal that lives mostly by killing and eating other animals

prey animal that is killed and eaten by another animal

species group of plants or animals that look and behave the same way

thrive live and grow successfully

threatened word that describes a group of animals whose numbers are decreasing, bringing the group close to endangerment

urban relating to the city

water table At a certain depth under Earth's surface, the ground is completely soaked with water. The borderline between the completely soaked ground and the ground above it is called the water table.

More Books to Read

Boraas, Tracy. *New Jersey.* Minnetonka, Minn.: Capstone Press, 2003.

Holtz, Eric Siegfried. *New Jersey: The Garden State.* Milwaukee: Gareth Stevens, 2002.

Nault, Jennifer. *A Guide to New Jersey.* New York City: Weigl Publishers, Inc., 2001.

Scholl, Elisabeth. *New Jersey.* Danbury, Conn.: Scholastic Library Publishing, 2002.

Stewart, Mark. *Uniquely New Jersey.* Chicago: Heinemann Library, 2003.

Index

About the Author

Mark Stewart makes his home in New Jersey. A graduate of Duke University with a degree in history, Stewart has authored more than 100 nonfiction titles for the school and library market. He and his wife Sarah have two daughters, Mariah and Rachel.